THE
SHOPPER'S
COMPANION

Text by Carol McD. Wallace
Design by Marleen Adlerblum

G.P. PUTNAM'S SONS
NEW YORK

G.P. Putnam's Sons
Publishers Since 1838
200 Madison Avenue
New York, NY 10016

Conceived and edited by
Alice van Straalen

Research
Melanie Greenup, Nancy Schreiber, Lawrence Saltzman

Shopping and Editorial Advisers
Pat Adrian, Maron Waxman

Printed in the United States of America
1 2 3 4 5 6 7 8 9 10

THE GOODS

Guide

THE BODY ESSENTIAL

Personal Care
Cosmetics, Nail Care, Perfumes and Colognes, Soaps, Toiletries

Pharmacy
Allergy Remedies, Eyeglasses, Over-the-Counter Medicines, Sunscreens, Vitamins

CLOTHING

Accessories
Belts, Handbags, Hats, Scarves, Umbrellas

Business Clothes

Casual Clothes

Children's Clothes

Evening Clothes

Jewelry

Lingerie/Sleepwear

Outerwear

Shoes and Boots

Sports Clothes

THE HOME

The Bath

Cleaning and Maintenance
Closets, Laundry, Workshop

Cooking and Dining
Cookware, Crystal and Glass, Cutlery, Dishes, Flatware, Kitchen Utensils

Decorating
Cabinetry, Flooring, Lighting, Mirrors, Paint and Wallpaper

Food

Furniture and Rugs

Gadgets

Home Appliances

Home Office
Calculators, Computer, Desk Accessories, Files and Storage

Linens
For Kitchen, Bath and Bedroom

Outdoor Living
Barbecue, Deck Chairs, Lawn Furniture, Swimming Pool

Window Dressing

PROFESSIONAL SERVICES

Childcare

Entertainment
Bartender, Caterer, Florist

Household
Carpenter, Electrician, Outdoor Maintenance, Plumber

Medical, Health and Dental

Personal Services
Barber, Hairdresser, Masseurs

Professional
Accountant, Investment Counselor, Insurance Agent, Lawyer, Travel Agent

Special Services
Piano Tuner, Tailor, Racket Restringer

SPECIAL OCCASIONS

Babies

Family Celebrations
Anniversaries, Birthdays, Graduations, Weddings

Gifts

Holidays
Christmas, Thanksgiving, etc.

Vacations

YOUR OWN TIME

Antiques and Collectibles

Books and Magazines

The Car

Children's World
Entertainment and Recreation

Electronics
Radio, Stereo, TV, VCR

Gardening

Health Club

Hobbies and Avocations
Crafts, Photography, Stamps

Pets

Sporting Goods

Tickets and Subscriptions
Ballet, Museums, Opera, Sports, Theater

Toys and Games

Personal Care

ONLY THE DMV KNOWS FOR SURE: Until the 1960s, hair color was listed on drivers' licenses. When a Long Island housewife, having become a blonde, updated her license, she was arrested for defacing the document. The judge threw the case out, saying, "Any woman has the right to change her mind and the color of her hair." Hair-care giant Clairol had a field day with this PR opportunity and put pressure on motor vehicle departments all over the country. Soon the hair color listing was stricken in many states, and also dropped from passports.

Personal Care

THE LANGUAGE OF *MOUCHES:* The next time you see a lady wearing a black velvet beauty spot, you might like to know what the placement traditionally says about her self-image.

• by the eye: *l'assassine* (killer) • on the forehead: *majestueuse* (majestic)
• on the cheek: *la galante* (courtesan) • near the lips: *la friponne* (rascal)

THE BODY ESSENTIAL

Personal Care

HIGH FINANCE: Years ago, Avon ladies in tribal villages on the Amazon never let lack of currency dent their sales. With help from their zone managers, they determined barter prices for their products, and cheerfully collected payment in the form of chickens, pigs, wood, or whatever was handy.

PURE LUCK: Ivory soap floats because in 1878 a Procter and Gamble employee left a vat of soap churning one day while he went out for lunch. The extra air whipped into the soap made it buoyant, but nobody at P and G realized what they had until the public began asking for "the soap that floats."

PHYSICIAN, HEAL THYSELF: A buyer for a New York department store was called on one day by fifteen or twenty salesmen for "hair restorers." Only two of them had full heads of hair.

Personal Care

Pharmacy

YOUR FULL-SERVICE PHARMACY I: A Montgomery Ward customer wrote in to order embalming fluid for her husband, who, though still alive, was looking "mighty peaked." She also asked for instructions: "Must I pour it down his throat just before he dies . . . ? Please rush."

YOUR FULL-SERVICE PHARMACY II: Wall Drug, in Wall, South Dakota (pop. 800), started attracting customers in 1936 by serving free ice water. Today coffee is still five cents a cup (refills free). The shop is a combination drugstore and tourist attraction, selling miniature Mount Rushmores and lariats along with the Bayer and Robitussin. It even contains a chapel. The proprietors have bought advertising as far away as Kenya to get publicity; fond customers have posted signs in locations like Shanghai and Lahore. In the summer tourist season, visitors to Wall Drug outnumber Wall's residents by 25 to 1.

Pharmacy

DOLLARS AND SCENTS: George Washington had his frivolous side. He liked his cologne (Caswell-Massey's No. 6) so much that he sent two bottles of the stuff to Lafayette. A later Francophile, Anna Gould (married to the Prince de Sagan), bought No. 6 by the gallon for sponge baths. It is still one of Caswell-Massey's best-sellers.

Pharmacy

Accessories

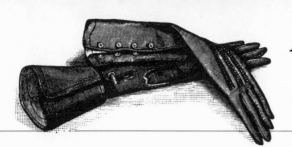

PRECIOUS: The minaudière, the beau monde's answer to the evening bag, is a large version of a gold Easter egg, fitted to contain a lady's necessities: comb, change, lipstick, powder. It was created by Louis Arpels, who spotted a customer, Florence Gould, using a long metal box as a purse. Her original minaudière had been a container for fifty Lucky Strike cigarettes.

Accessories

Accessories

CONCEALED WEAPONS: In 1913, the State Children's Court in Adelaide, Australia, prosecuted nineteen women for wearing unprotected hat pins. Said the magistrate to one: "It seems to me that the hat pin you are wearing now is a very long one. Is it used for any other purpose?" Replied the defendant, hotly: "No, but it might be."

Accessories

BRINGING HOME THE OFFICE: Harry Houdini had a pocket watch made by Tiffany and Company whose chain was formed of tiny handcuffs.

Business Clothes

QUEEN-SIZE: The London department store Howell and James supplied Queen Victoria with silk to be made up into dresses. She required twenty- four yards for each dress, a measurement the buyer who delivered the goods termed "very ample."

Business Clothes

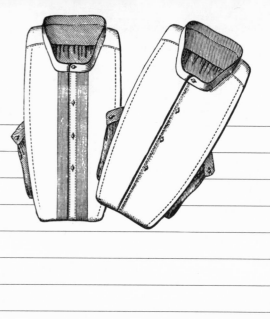

POSTAGE PAID, FREEPORT, MAINE: L. L. Bean's service is so prompt and reliable that in 1973 they received a rush order for boots and sturdy shirts—from the Israeli army.

Business Clothes

Casual Clothes

KNEECAPPING: In the 1960s, Coco Chanel was asked if she approved of women's exposing their thighs in the new short skirts. "Thighs—of course," she answered. "But knees—never!"

Casual Clothes

Casual Clothes

A DELICATE CONDITION: In the early years of this century, impending motherhood was looked on as something to be hidden from prying public eyes. The Lane Bryant department store didn't feel it could place a newspaper ad for its maternity dresses until 1911. When it finally did, the entire stock was sold out by the end of the day.

THE LITTLE PEOPLE: By its own reckoning, Mattel, Inc., produces more women's apparel than any other company in the world. Its best customer, Barbie, is eleven and a half inches tall.

Casual Clothes

Children's Clothes

KIDDIE KONSUMERS: Who are the advertising world's strongest allies? Not the ones with the checkbooks. Dr. Frances Horwith, of the 1950s TV show "Ding Dong School," once warned, "Never underestimate the buying power of a child under seven. He has brand loyalty and the determination to see that his parents purchase the product of his choice."

Children's Clothes

_____
_____
_____
_____
_____
_____
_____
_____
_____
_____
_____
_____
_____
_____
_____
_____
_____
_____

SEED MONEY: The ubiquitous Benetton stores—4,300 all over the world—sell not only clothes for teenagers and fashion-conscious adults, but also a line called 012, for kids. (The young Princes of Wales have been photographed in clothes sporting the 012 logo.) The company was founded with less than twenty dollars, raised from the sale of Luciano Benetton's accordion and his brother Carlo's bicycle.

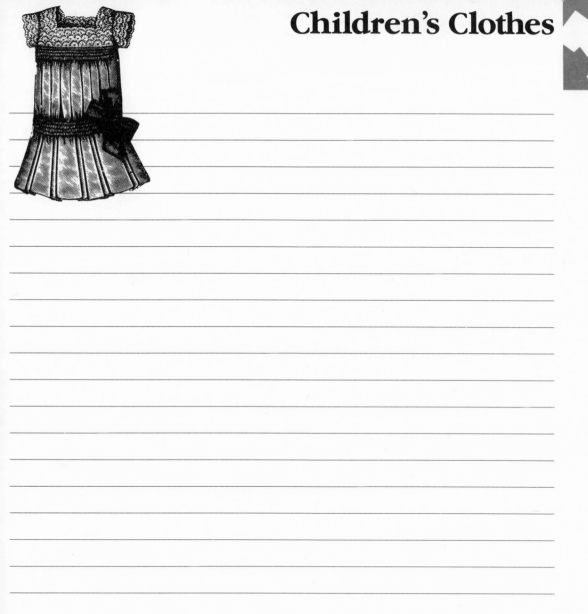

Children's Clothes

Evening Clothes

BASIC: Until the beginning of the nineteenth century, men dressed as flamboyantly as women for special occasions. Then English dandy Beau Brummell began wearing strictly black clothes in the evening, setting a fashion that still prevails.

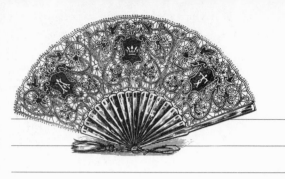

Evening Clothes

SAVING FACE: I. Magnin's once had a customer who, deeply admiring the sequined evening dresses of Norman Norell, had the buyer take her measurements so that he could automatically send her each sequined Norell that came in. For three years, each shipment was answered with a thank-you note and a check. Then, though the checks kept coming, the notes stopped. Several years later, the buyer ran into the woman unexpectedly, and instantly understood. She had stopped writing notes because she had stopped wearing the dresses. But paying for them was less painful than admitting she'd put on dozens of pounds—and now had much more generous measurements.

Jewelry

BAIT AND SWITCH: The two largest cut precious stones in the world are diamonds, part of Britain's Crown Jewels; one weighs 530.2 carats, the other 317.4 carats. They were both cut from the Cullinan Diamond, found in the Transvaal in 1905. Uncut, it weighed 3,106 carats. The Transvaal government voted to give the stones to King Edward VII of England, a conciliatory gesture after the Boer War. The stones were insured, and detectives were hired to guard a counterfeit stone in the captain's safe on the steamer voyage to England. Meanwhile, the real stones went alone, via parcel post.

TRIUMPH OF VIRTUE: An elderly gentleman went to his wife's favorite jeweler, Cartier, to commission something special. Louis Cartier complied, setting sapphires, emeralds, diamonds, and rubies in solid gold to produce an extremely luxurious chastity belt.

Lingerie/Sleepwear

A NEW ERA DAWNS: On May 6, 1911, what is purportedly the first national ad for men's underwear ran in the *Saturday Evening Post*. Drawn by the *Post*'s artist (and creator of the glamorous Arrow Shirt man), J. C. Leyendecker, it featured a union suit with the patented Kenosha Klosed Krotch.

LEFT LUGGAGE: In the early 1920s, mothers were still insisting that their daughters wear corsets, and always checked for the telltale whalebone as girls went out for the evening. Daring debutantes, however, simply removed the offending undergarments at parties and left them in the cloakroom, where they sometimes outnumbered the coats.

Outerwear

_____

_____

_____

_____

_____

_____

_____

_____

_____

_____

_____

_____

_____

_____

_____

_____

_____

_____

REPUBLICAN IMAGERY: Painter Jacques Louis David designed uniforms for the five officials of the French Directoire, who governed France after the Reign of Terror. David's costume for the anti-aristocratic ruling class included silk stockings, a plumed hat, a "Roman" sword, a lace collar, and a long, heavily embroidered cape in a brilliant revolutionary red.

_____

_____

_____

_____

_____

_____

_____

TRIAL BY FIRE: In 1910, the British clothiers Burberry introduced a new coat made of their special weatherproof cotton. Called the "Tielocken" (presumably because it fastened with a "strap-and-buckle" instead of buttons), it was soon adapted to the needs of officers in World War I with additional epaulets and D rings. This version was so popular that some half million officers wore it during the war. Hence its nickname—the "trench coat."

Shoes and Boots

WORTH THE TRIP: The world's first shoe museum opened in Schonenwerd, Switzerland, in 1942. Founded by the shoe manufacturer Bally, its collection comprises shoe-abilia (a Tanagra figurine, fifth century B.C., of a goddess removing her shoes) as well as outstanding examples of the shoemaker's art, from Egyptian grass sandals to a shoe worn by Pope Pius VII at Napoleon's coronation as emperor.

Shoes and Boots

TWO LEFT FEET: The shoes sold in American country stores in the eighteenth century were identical for left and right feet; it was up to the buyer to break them in as a pair. When the first shoes built differently for each foot were invented, they were caustically called "crooked shoes."

Shoes and Boots

WHAT ABOUT THE PUMPKIN?: For a 1925 production of *Cinderella* starring Gloria Swanson, Steuben Glass made six pairs of glass slippers, patterned on a pair of Miss Swanson's own pumps. They were featured in advertising, and in close-ups. It is not recorded that Miss Swanson ever walked in them.

FIT TO BE TIED: In an enthusiastic misuse of new technology, some shoe stores in the 1930s installed X-ray machines to check the fit of their customers' shoes.

Shoes and Boots

Sports Clothes

CLOTHING

Sports Clothes

Q.E.D.: The new American game of base-ball was slow to generate a consistent uni-form. In 1882, the Detroit Wolverines spent a season wearing jerseys and caps that identified their positions: first base was red and white stripes, pitcher was sky blue, shortstop was brown. They not only were ugly, they were superfluous: once the play-ers were on the field, they could be identi-fied by their positions anyway.

The Bath

The Bath

BUT WHAT ABOUT CLEANLINESS AND GODLINESS?: Though the Romans bathed frequently and their public baths dotted Europe in the medieval period (Charles the Bold even took a silver bathtub on military campaigns), bathing fell out of favor after the sixteenth century, partly because of the supposed risk of syphilis spreading through water. As late as the end of the eighteenth century, Parisians regarded baths as medication, and rarely submitted to this treatment more than once a year.

_____

_____

_____

_____

_____

_____

_____

_____

_____

_____

_____

_____

_____

_____

_____

_____

_____

_____

_____

_____

_____

_____

_____

_____

_____

_____

_____

_____

The Bath

TWICE A DAY: These are the ingredients that make up toothpaste: water; chalk (the abrasive factor); titanium dioxide (whitener, the stuff in white latex paint); glycerine glycol, seaweed and paraffin oil (for texture); detergent (to make bubbles); peppermint oil and saccharin (for that fresh flavor); and formaldehyde to keep the concoction from spoiling.

COMFORTS OF HOME: In aristocratic seventeenth-century France, the bathroom did not exist. Bathing was not customary, and the call of nature was answered casually. The corridors at Versailles, for example, reeked.

The Bath

Cleaning and Maintenance

THE HOME

Cleaning and Maintenance

I'LL TAKE THE CLOSET: In 1958, *Cosmopolitan* magazine ran an article predicting that by 1982, American women would be relieved of all housework except pushing a few buttons. Inventions to lighten the work load would include: the ultrasonic closet that shook dirt off clothes; the robot vacuum cleaner that lived in a hole in the wall and when summoned negotiated its way around the floor unaided; an ultraviolet ray that would zap germs from guests on the doorstep; and an unspecified device to emit cooking smells, since new speedy culinary techniques would have eliminated that homey touch.

Cooking and Dining

Cooking and Dining

COOKING FROM SCRATCH: The kitchen at the Waldorf-Astoria uses more than half a ton of chicken, beef, and veal bones *every day* to make its soups and stocks.

Cooking and Dining

QUALITY CONTROL: Small pellets of plastic arrive by the railroad car load at Tupperware plants, and are tested before being unloaded. Samples are taken from each car, heated, and placed in a jar with half a saltine. The jar is sealed. When it is opened hours later, the saltine had better not taste or smell of plastic. If it does, the whole carload of pellets is rejected.

Cooking and Dining

Decorating

SPOTTY SUCCESS: After Macy's introduced a very popular line of innovatively colored kitchen accessories, an executive ordered a further improvement: polka dots. The dotted line has been discontinued.

Decorating

AND THAT'S THAT: "Broadloom" (as in carpets) says nothing about weave or quality. It only means that the carpet is at least six feet wide, or woven on a broad loom.

Decorating

WHERE YOUR TREASURE IS:
In 1958, *House and Garden* suggested that its readers tile their garages and add house plants and porch furniture to the lawn mower and snow shovel. The editorial reasoning: cars of the late 1950s were so beautiful that their owners would want to spend leisure time looking at them. Carbon monoxide poisoning was not, apparently, a concern.

Food

IT ROSE: When the United States sent its Vanguard rocket into space in 1958, the payload included some Fleischmann's Active Dry Yeast, to discern the effect of space travel on live organisms.

Food

Food

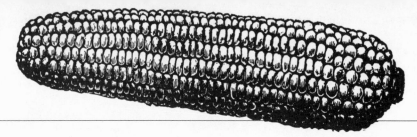

GREAT EXPECTATIONS: In April of 1912, the National Biscuit Company alerted its salesmen to the debut of three new cookies. Immense popularity was anticipated for the Mother Goose ("a rich, high class biscuit") and the Veronese ("a delicious, hard, sweet biscuit"). Also introduced was the Oreo ("two beautifully embossed, chocolate-flavored wafers with a rich cream filling").

HORROR SHOW: A Scottish firm of candy makers claimed great success in 1983 with their "Skull Crushers," white chocolate skulls that, when bitten, oozed a bright red filling.

Furniture and Rugs

Furniture and Rugs

PREFERRED SEATING: Only Louis XIV, of all the folk at Versailles, was allowed to sit in a chair with arms. Chairs with backs were reserved for his immediate circle; stools, for certain levels of the aristocracy. The lower ranks relied on folding stools without padding. But since the palace contained only 1,325 of these (when its population was several thousand), most courtiers simply stood.

Furniture and Rugs

SLEEP TIGHT: Medieval beds, often as large as ten feet square, were scaled to accommodate many sleepers. The famous Great Bed of Ware could hold eight.

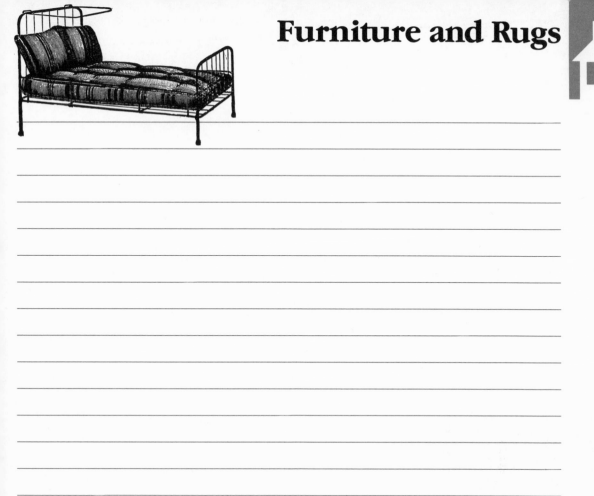

Furniture and Rugs

Gadgets

GRACIOUS LIVING: Standard equipment in the genteel nineteenth-century household included an egg decapitator (to avoid the crude act of cutting off the top of the egg with a knife), a table blowpipe (to extinguish the fire under a chafing dish), and lazy tongs (long extendable tongs to pick up small items from the floor; heaven forbid one should have to stoop!).

Gadgets

NICE TRY: Thomas Edison's first patent was for an electrical vote recorder. Nobody wanted it.

Gadgets

THE **H**OME

Home Appliances

ANY ONE WILL DO: Inventor Guglielmo Marconi was instructed to set up communications between Queen Victoria's retreat at Osborne House and the royal yacht. When Marconi, checking the wires, walked across her private garden, she was incensed at his *lèse majesté,* and commanded, "Get another electrician."

Home Appliances

Home Appliances

_____

_____

_____

_____

_____

_____

_____

_____

_____

_____

_____

_____

SUCKING UP II: The inventor of the vacuum cleaner, H. Cecil Booth, got his idea for a suction cleaner from a device that purported to _blow_ dust away. Booth apparently instantly realized that _sucking_ would work better, and proved this by inhaling several mouthfuls of dust from his office carpet. Soon he had a product on the market, though it was so large that the body rode along the street and a suction hose was passed in through windows of houses to be serviced. The ultimate accolade came when Booth's suction cleaner was chosen to clean Westminster Abbey before Edward VII's coronation.

Home Appliances

Home Office

MARATHON PLUS: The average pencil has enough lead in it to draw a thirty-five-mile line.

Home Office

LOOK MOM, NO BLOTS: The American fondness for pencils dates from the Civil War, when soldiers found them handier than quill pens for writing letters from the front.

SECOND THOUGHTS: It isn't the rubber that gets rid of mistakes. Pencil erasers contain pumice, which actually abrades away a tiny layer of paper and the lead with it.

Home Office

Linens

DON'T LET THE BEDBUGS BITE: The average double bed harbors some two million mites, tiny insects that live on the thousands of dead skin flakes we shed every minute. So small that they weren't discovered until 1965, they have since been found sixteen thousand feet up Mt. Everest and deep in the Pacific. Unlike other insects that live in bedding, they are not carnivorous.

Linens

EFFICIENCY EXPERT: Prime Minister Gladstone, like many other Britons, used a hot water bottle to keep warm at night. His, however, was filled with sugared tea, which he drank upon awakening in the morning.

Outdoor Living

THE HOME

NO MORE ROTISSERIE GRILLING: Abercrombie and Fitch sells a "sun table" for five thousand dollars that lights the tan-worshiper's body from top and bottom simultaneously.

Outdoor Living

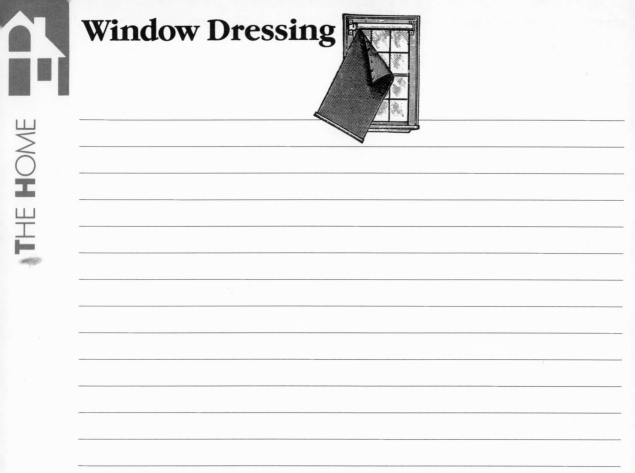

Window Dressing

ISN'T THAT HANDY: Aluminum, discovered in the nineteenth century, was considered very precious: the emperor of France replaced his silver cutlery with a set of pure aluminum, while Congress wanted to place a slab of the metal on top of the Washington Monument. In addition to its appealing lightness and shiny surface, aluminum has a unique property. It repairs itself, coating nicks and gouges with a new smooth skin that inhibits rusting. Thus aluminum's appropriateness for high-friction spots like window frames.

Window Dressing

LET THE SUNSHINE IN: The Dutch town houses of the seventeenth century were Europe's first row houses, with shared side walls. Because the cross walls bore no weight, they could be pierced with large windows, letting floods of light (think of Vermeer) into the rooms. Large panes of glass were awkward to open and close, so the canny Dutch invented the double-hung sash window. Of course, large windows on the street meant a certain loss of privacy, hence another Dutch invention: window curtains.

Childcare

CUSTOMER RELATIONS: Rich's, the Atlanta-based department store, used to send a card to every child born in a Georgia hospital.

Childcare

Childcare

SAY GOOD NIGHT: Caroline Kennedy's favorite bedtime stories were the tales her father told her about a white whale that lived on socks. When the family was cruising on the presidential yacht, Kennedy felt the story needed a boost of reality, and made a guest, Franklin D. Roosevelt, Jr., feed the whale with his own socks.

Entertainment

AGE OF STANDARDIZATION: Hundreds of years ago, bareback riders realized that it was easiest for them to keep their balance on horses that were galloping around a ring about forty two feet in diameter. Modern science tells us that centrifugal force makes the difference—and therefore all circus rings are this size.

Household

PENTAGON CALLING: The Avon cosmetics sales force numbers around 1.4 million representatives worldwide. For comparison, there are some 781,000 members of the United States Army.

Household

Household

TROMPE-L'OEIL: Wallpaper was originally the poor man's tapestry. Printed by the method used to make playing cards and called *domino,* it was widely found in modest houses all over eighteenth-century France. Even great houses often had a small closet that was papered, and the attic walls were always hung with paper, often in a black-and-white stripe that would be the height of chic today.

WHO'D A THUNK IT?: The best way to clean
a freezer is with a plastic car de-icer.

Household

PROFESSIONAL SERVICES

Medical, Health and Dental

CARTER'S LITTLE LIVER PILLS
For HEADACHE,
For DIZZINESS,
For BILIOUSNESS,
For TORPID LIVER,
For CONSTIPATION,
For SALLOW SKIN,
For the COMPLEXION.

CHARGE!: Fitness equipment in bygone years included "shocking coils," a gadget that administered an electrical shock and was touted to cure gout, lumbago, constipation, insomnia, and neuralgia. The level of current was adjustable for anything from a tingle to a jolt.

Medical, Health and Dental

Medical, Health and Dental

Medical, Health and Dental

CORN MEAL

HOUSE CALL: The doctor who delivered
Dolly Parton was paid for his services with
a sack of cornmeal.

Personal Services

Personal Services

GRAPHIC: Barbers' poles were originally solid red, with a little pot hanging underneath. The red was for blood, since barbers performed surgery; the pot signified that they also "cupped" or bled clients. The familiar white stripes, added in the eighteenth century, stood for linen bandages.

Professional

RISKY BUSINESS: Lloyd's of London has insured such items as Betty Grable's legs, Jimmy Durante's nose, and flamenco dancer Jose Greco's skintight trousers. They turned down the back teeth of an acrobat (who hung by her mouth during her act) and a young lady's virginity.

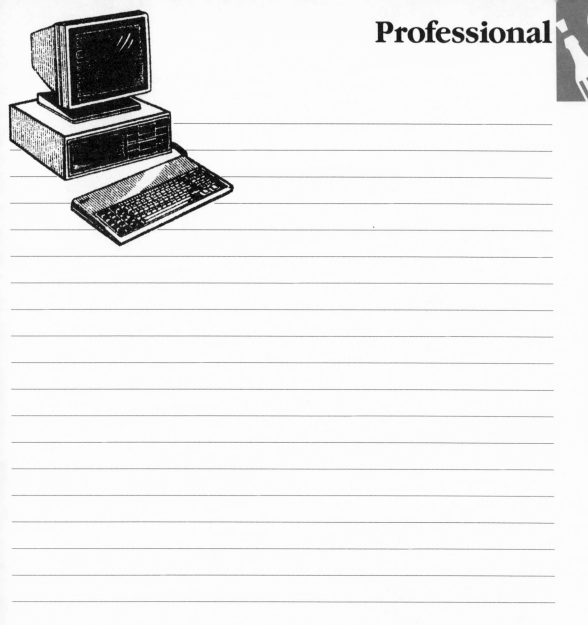

Special Services

PROFESSIONAL SERVICES

CLEAN UP YOUR ACT: Sign on a tattoo parlor/barber's in lower Manhattan a number of years ago: "Shave 10¢, Haircut 20¢, Black Eyes Made Natural."

Special Services

Babies

FOR THE CHILD WHO HAS EVERYTHING: Baby blankets are a classic gift for the new-born. Madeleine Astor had one made for her son John Jacob Astor VI—in mink.

Babies

AND BELLS ON THEIR TOES?: In 1919, some 600,000 American babies wore gold-filled rings from Woolworth's.

OH, HOW . . . LARGE: F.A.O Schwarz has initiated a computerized infant and children's gift registry to prevent duplication on Schwarz specialties like, say, Koko the Gorilla—who is life-sized.

Family Celebrations

POTLATCH: The practice of displaying wedding gifts emerged during the nineteenth century as the wedding celebration became a vehicle for conspicuous display of wealth. It was also necessary to hire someone to guard the display. The richer the families, the more presents and the more guards. When Henry Ford II married Anne McDonnell, it took sixteen people to watch over the loot, which included a custom-built Ford with its own chauffeur.

Family Celebrations

Family Celebrations

SECRECY ACT: The design team of David and Elizabeth Emanuel noticed, as they were working on Lady Diana Spencer's wedding dress, that their garbage bins kept disappearing. They assumed that the contents were being stolen to provide clues about the top secret project, so they made sure that any scraps of fabric thrown away were dead white. The real scraps from the dress, which was ivory, were carefully burned.

Family Celebrations

Gifts

A LITTLE LIGHT READING: Lewis Carroll's *Alice in Wonderland* was a great success, and one of its admirers was Queen Victoria. She had the author notified that she would be pleased to read copies of any of his other works. Shortly afterward, Her Majesty received his *Syllabus of Plane Geometry*.

MUSICAL TASTE: Available to take home from the Liberace Museum in Las Vegas: a music box in the shape of a white baby grand piano, complete with candelabra. It plays "Somewhere My Love."

Gifts

A GIRL'S BEST FRIEND: Nineteenth-century opera diva Adelina Patti made a very successful European tour and was asked by a critic which of her numerous royal fans she liked best. Thoughtfully, she answered, "The Czar Alexander gives the best jewelry."

WHAT ABOUT THE SAUCE?: One of the most elaborate April Fool's hoaxes ever appeared on British television: Italian farmers were filmed harvesting spaghetti from trees.

Holidays

MOVABLE FEAST: Thanksgiving used to be the last Thursday in November. But since Christmas shopping doesn't swing into high gear until the turkey is eaten, a November 30 Thanksgiving could mean a short selling season. So in 1939, the head of the F. and R. Lazarus department stores mounted a campaign to proclaim Thanksgiving the *fourth* Thursday in November. He persuaded store owners to lobby, and in 1941, Congress made the proposal law. Now Thanksgiving never falls later than November 28.

Vagations

COLOR COORDINATED: When decorator Elsie de Wolfe first went to Greece, she was as struck by her first sight of the Acropolis as most tourists—but for a different reason. She exclaimed, "It's beige! My color!"

NATURAL WONDER: Maine's second-biggest tourist attraction is L. L. Bean, surpassed only by the Atlantic Ocean.

YOUR OWN TIME

HE BOUGHT FLEET INSURANCE: Liberace owned more cars (forty-eight) than pianos (forty-two).

Antiques and Collectibles

BIG BACKING: Denmark's Royal Copenhagen porcelain was founded with financial support from the dowager queen Juliane Marie in 1775. She is credited with the trademark of three wavy blue lines (standing for the seas around Denmark) beneath a crown. The company's most famous china pattern, Flora Danica, was commissioned by Crown Prince Frederik in 1789. It is still produced.

Antiques and Collectibles

YOUR OWN TIME

A MERE BAGATELLE: Malcolm Forbes' collection of Faberge items is rivaled only by those of the Soviet government and the queen of England. One of his early purchases was a cigarette case bought for his wife, Roberta. The scholar who later catalogued Forbes' collection dismissed it as "the kind of thing that the Czar gave to the station-master on state visits."

Books and Magazines

YOUR OWN TIME

Books and Magazines

Books and Magazines

GIVING GOOD WEIGHT: Dorothy Canfield of Book-of-the-Month Club once reminisced about a blockbuster of the 1930s: "It was chosen with a little difficulty, because some of the characterization was not very authentic or convincing. . . . One of the judges said, 'Well, people may not like it very much, but nobody can deny that it gives a lot of reading for your money.' " "It" was *Gone With the Wind*.

Books and Magazines

The Car

SECRET WEAPON: Glamorous T. E. Lawrence, one of the few Britons ever to refuse the Victoria Cross, led the Arabs in a revolt against the Turks during World War I. For mobility on the sands, he relied on a fleet of armored Rolls-Royces: "In the desert a Rolls was prized above rubies," he later wrote.

The Car

SEMIOTICS OF DETROIT: One manifestation of American confidence in the 1950s was the elaborate styling of the automobiles, notably the phenomenon of fins. Originally vertical extrusions, they gradually stretched out horizontally, reaching their winglike apotheosis on the 1959 Chevrolet. It was a far cry from the original finny inspiration, the double tails of the P-38 bomber.

Children's World

AT LEAST HE DIDN'T CALL IT HILDEGARDE: An Austrian candy manufacturer named Leon Hirshfield invented a chewy chocolate log and decided to name it after his girlfriend. Thus, the Tootsie Roll.

Children's World

Children's World

AND THEY *MEAN GREAT:* Tonka trucks are made by the Mound Metalcraft Company, founded in Mound, Minnesota. "Tonka," the word emblazoned on the trucks, means "great" in the Dakota Sioux language. To emphasize the toys' sturdiness (they are made of steel), one 1970s advertisement featured a two-ton elephant stepping on a Tonka dump truck. The truck did not dent.

TRUTH IN ADVERTISING: The term "Crayola," invented by the wife of one of the manufacturers in 1903, combined the French for "stick of color" (*craie*) with the word particle meaning "oil" (ola). The biggest box of Crayolas purports to contain seventy-two crayons. In fact, it holds seventy-three.

YOUR OWN TIME

Electronics

YOUR OWN TIME

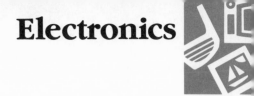

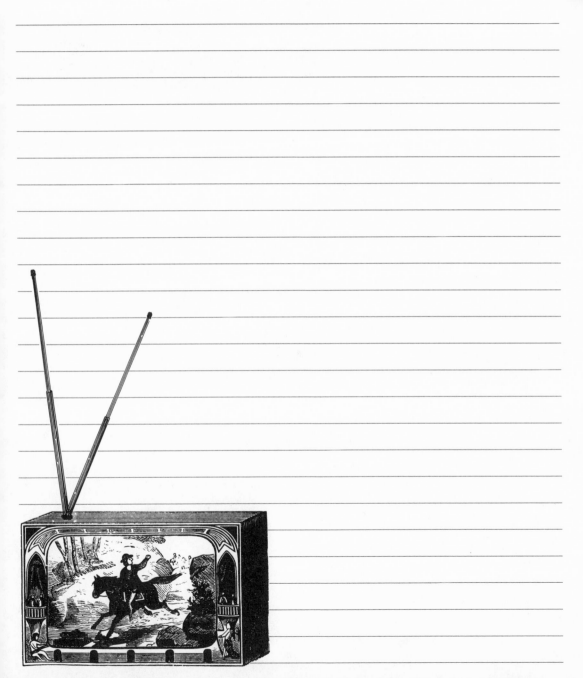

Electronics

CALL WAITING: When you dial an international call, there is a delay before you start to hear the reassuring clicks that tell you your call is getting through. The delay is the amount of time it takes a microwave to travel from earth to a satellite and back, at the speed of light.

TUNE IN: In 1959, America's 44 million families possessed some 56 million cars, 50 million televisions, and 143 million radios, or an average 3.25 radios per household.

Gardening

JACK OF ALL TRADES: In the summer of 1924, Winston Churchill was devoting himself to the life of a country gentleman. His family had just moved into the estate of Chartwell, and though the grounds included one lake, Churchill wanted another. A pond was excavated, and water from a spring was diverted into it. But both bodies of water were too muddy and weed-choked for swimming. So the statesman decided to consign one lake to the wildfowl, drain the second, and dig a third, which would have a waterproof bottom and a concrete dike. He hired workmen and pressed his bodyguard into service, eagerly shoveling mud alongside them. The bottom of the third pond leaked. The dike was unsteady. Churchill finally put a swimming pool up by the house, and turned his energies to bricklaying.

Gardening

OVERRULED: Louis XIV so loved flowers that, when France was at peace with Holland, he would order four million tulips annually from Dutch nurseries for Versailles. He insisted that they be placed in parterres in front of the palace, over the objections of his famous landscape architect, Le Notre, who hated blooming plants.

YOUR OWN TIME

Health Club

MIDTOWN PASTORALE: When Rockefeller Center's skating rink opened in 1936, it was the first outdoor ice skating arena in New York City, and one of the first in the country. In spite of its urban setting—surrounded by skyscrapers, overlooked by the Prometheus Fountain, floodlit at night—and highly touted equipment to keep the artificial ice groomed, it was nostalgically named the Skating Pond.

Health Club

Hobbies and Avocations

YOUR OWN TIME

Hobbies and Avocations

ESOTERICA: Businesslike request from Tupper Lake, New York, received by Macy's some years ago: "Will you kindly advise me if you have any dead horses for sale. . . . Please quote me your lowest price, on receipt of which I will send you my check and give you shipping instructions." Businesslike response: "We are consumed with curiosity as to just what you expected to do with a dead horse. . . . Our limited knowledge would lead us to believe that the prospect of a dead horse is much greater at Tupper Lake than it is at Broadway and 34th Street."

Hobbies and Avocations

PENNY WISE: Nineteenth-century financier Hetty Green was also a famous miser. Legend has it that she bought some dress fabric at Benjamin Altman's department store and found a flaw. She took it back, and Altman offered her a replacement or her money back. She was so pleased at his response (not standard retail policy at the time) that she introduced him to her bankers and offered to guarantee any loans he might need.

Hobbies and Avocations

YOUR OWN TIME

Pets

BUT DO THEY DO WINDOWS?: A Philadelphia newspaper ran an ad in 1877 that parodied the proclamations of Wanamaker's new department stores. One offer in this satire were oysters that had been trained to sit still in a cool cellar; when the cook whistled, "the educated bivalves [would] come into the kitchen by the dozens, open themselves, and jump into the stewing pan."

WHO NEEDS FIVE FINGERS?: The elephant's trunk, which contains forty thousand muscles, is so dextrous that some pachyderms can use them to untie knots.

Sporting Goods

FITNESS FRENZY: According to *Harper's Index*, 70 percent of the Americans who own running shoes do no running in them.

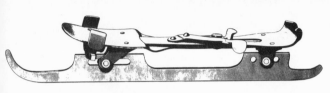

Sporting Goods

THE REST IS HISTORY: In 1910, Leon Leonwood Bean had the brilliant notion of stitching a flexible leather boot top to a waterproof rubber bottom. After he and his friends tried out the boots in the woods over a winter, he felt confident enough to offer them for sale. In 1912, ninety holders of Maine hunting licenses bought Maine Hunting Shoes. All ninety pairs were returned because the rubber bottoms were too flimsy and separated from the uppers. Bean promptly replaced each pair.

Tickets and Subscriptions

FEISTY: Nineteenth-century athlete Sir Claude Champion performed several feats of courage and endurance. He was the first European to swim the Nile Rapids, he and a partner were the first people to cross the North Sea in a balloon, and at age sixty-one he walked the forty-five miles from Essex to London, for no greater incentive than a bet of two shillings sixpence. He also believed that boxing was the ultimate test of a man's character, and applicants for jobs at his country house had to put on the gloves with him as part of the interview.

Tickets and Subscriptions

Toys and Games

WHAT'S WRONG WITH CHESS?: Each astronaut of the Apollo 8 space mission took along Silly Putty in a sterling silver eggshell. The Silly Putty was supposed to keep their tools from floating around during the weightless portions of the trip. And, of course, to keep them from getting bored.

CAPITALIST TOOL: The game of Monopoly is not sold in the Soviet Union because it's ideologically taboo. However, at a recent American National Exhibition in Moscow, six games were on display. All six were stolen.

Toys and Games

Toys and Games

CHECK: Chess originated in India and came to the West sometime in the seventh century. The chess pieces are thought to represent the four parts of an ancient Hindu army: elephants, horses, chariots, and foot soldiers.

YOUR OWN TIME

SOURCES AND SUPPLIERS

ABCD

NAME:

NAME:

NAME:

WHO'S THE FAIREST: In 1848, the first full-length mirrors to appear in an American store were installed in the second-floor Ladies' Parlor of A. T. Stewart's Marble Dry Goods Palace in New York. Other Stewart innovations: fashion shows, firm prices (as opposed to bargaining), and honesty (the boss instructed his clerks, "Never cheat a customer, even if you can").

NAME:

ABCD

NAME:

NAME:

NAME:

NAME:

ABCD

NAME:

NAME:

NAME:

NAME:

NAME:

NAME:

EPONYMITY: The first enclosed shopping mall outside of Minnesota (where weather made the enclosure essential) was in Delaware Township, New Jersey. It was so successful that the town took on its name, and became Cherry Hill.

NAME:

NAME:

EFGH

NAME:

NAME:

NAME:

NAME:

EFGH

NAME:

NAME:

NAME:

SELF-HELP: America's first self-service stores were Tennessee's chain of Piggly Wiggly food stores, founded in 1916. Customers entered through a turnstile and followed a path through the aisles that displayed all the wares the store had to offer. Sales clerks were unnecessary.

EFGH

NAME:

_____   _____

_____   _____

_____   _____

_____   _____

_____

STAND STILL!: Until the mid-twenties, mannequins
for shop windows were made of wax, and in extreme   _____
heat were liable to lose their poses by melting. The
innovation of the twenties was to make them out of   _____
papier-mâché and use horsehair for their wags.
_____

_____

_____

NAME:

_____   _____

_____   _____

_____   _____

_____   _____

NAME:

_____   _____

_____   _____

_____   _____

_____   _____

_____

EFGH

NAME:

NAME:

NAME:

NAME:

IJKL

NAME:

NAME:

NAME:

NAME:

NAME:

TRY, TRY AGAIN: In 1845, Bostonian Rowland H. Macy closed an account book. Against his sales for May 13 ("1 pr. hose, .25, 2 papers of pins @ 8¢, .16") totaling $.64, he had outlays of $4.10 ("Cash to milk-man"). On the next page, he wrote, "I have worked Two Years for Nothing. Damn. Damn. damn. damn." Thirteen years later, he opened a new store in New York.

IJKL

IN HIS OTHER LIFE: L. Frank Baum had two books published in 1900. One was called *The Wonderful Wizard of Oz.* The other was called *The Art of Decorating Dry Goods Windows and Interiors.*

NAME:

NAME:

NAME:

IJKL

NAME:

NAME:

NAME:

NAME:

MNOPQ

NAME:

_____

NAME:

_____

NAME:

_____

NAME:

_____

FATHER OF JUNK MAIL: Benjamin Franklin's job as America's first postmaster general wasn't his only connection to the post office. He also issued, in 1744, a list of six hundred books for sale through the post, possibly the country's first example of mail order.

NAME:

NAME:

NAME:

MNOPQ

NAME:

NAME:

SCHOOL FOR SHOPKEEPERS: Bettlebeck's dry goods store in Newark, New Jersey, though not itself famous, had three salesclerks who went on to greater things. They were Lyman Bloomingdale (of Bloomingdale's), Benjamin Altman (of Altman's), and Abraham Abraham (of Abraham and Straus).

NAME:

NAME:

MNOPQ

NAME:

NAME:

NAME:

NAME:

RSTU

NAME:

NAME:

NAME:

AN IDEA WHOSE TIME HAS COME: Some nine-teenth-century department stores offered, among other amenities, "silence rooms" for "nerve-frazzled shoppers."

NAME:

NAME:

NAME:

NAME:

RSTU

NAME:

NAME:

NAME:

NAME:

NAME:

_____
_____
_____
_____
_____
_____

FIVE-FINGER DISCOUNT: In 1885, a lady in London was caught with forty-two handkerchiefs, twenty-four and a half yards of velvet, two pairs of gloves, and a bunch of ribbons hidden under her crinoline.

NAME:

NAME:

NAME:

VWXYZ

NAME:

NAME:

THE CUSTOMER'S RIGHT: Rich's department store in Atlanta has an extremely liberal return policy. They will accept anything the customer cares to return, no matter how old it is or what shape it is in. They have taken back altered clothes, items from other stores, a thirty-year-old pair of shoes—and a dead canary.

NAME:

NAME:

NAME:

NAME:

VWXYZ

NAME:

NAME:

NAME:

NAME:

NAME:

DID THEY GET PAID?: Liberty of London provided decorating services for customers as far afield as India and South Africa. They were in the middle of a job for Archduke Franz Ferdinand of Austria at the time of his assassination, the event that sparked World War I.

NAME:

NAME:

CLAIRVOYANT: In an effort to add some class to its wares, Sears, Roebuck offered a line of very fashionable dresses in its 1917 catalog. Their designer, English aristocrat Lady Duff Gordon, called one of them "I'll Be Coming Back to You." Two were sold: two came back.

NAME:

#

NAME:

#

NAME:

#

NAME:

#

NAME:

#

NAME:

#

NAME:

#

NAME:

#

NAME: _____

_____

_____

_____

_____

_____

NAME: _____

_____

_____

_____

_____

_____

NAME: _____

_____

_____

_____

_____

_____

CREDITABLE: In eighteenth-century London, silver coins were in short supply, and shopkeepers had to be on the watch for counterfeit or broken coins. Customers' currency was often checked on scales to make sure it came up to full weight. Because dealing with cash was so cumbersome, most shops offered credit and allowed bills to run for as long as a year.

NAME: _____

_____

_____

_____

_____

_____

NAME: _____

_____

_____

_____

_____

_____

NAME: _____

_____

_____

_____

_____

_____

NAME: _____

_____

_____

_____

_____

_____

THERE WILL ALWAYS BE AN ENGLAND: An enterprising Washington radio station called a number of foreign ambassadors in the winter of 1948 to ask what they wanted for Christmas, then broadcast their (unedited) answers. The French ambassador wanted world peace. The Russian emissary requested freedom from imperialism. The British envoy, Sir Oliver Franks, said politely, "It's very kind of you to ask. I'd quite like a box of crystallized fruit."

Aloe vera	*Earmuffs*
Andirons	*Earring rack*
Anna Karenina	*Eau de cologne*
Assortment of coffees	*Elegant address book*
Attaché case	*Eucalyptus branches*
Back brush	*Facial*
Basket of soaps	*Fifty-dollar book club gift certificate*
Bayberry candles	*Field glasses for sports buff*
Beach towel	*Fishing creel*
Belt buckle	*Flower vase*
Bicycle (mobile or stationary)	
Bicycle basket	*Green muffler*
Binoculars	
Blue and white checked cotton napkins	*Hair ornaments*
Book of nursery rhymes	*Hammock*
Bottle of champagne	*Handmade quilt*
Brunch in bed	*Handmuffs*
Bubble bath	*Handwarmer*
Bulletin board	*Heating tray*
	Heavy-duty chef's apron
Cane	*Honeys and jams*
Cashmere gloves	*Hot plate*
Ceramic water pitcher	
Challis shawl	*Ice bucket*
Chinese dishware	*Imported mustards*
China doll	*Insulated knapsack*
Coasters	
Coatrack	*Jump rope*
Concert series subscription	
Coral paperweight	
Croquet set	
Dictionary	
Dinosaur sweatshirt	
Dinner for two	
Doll carriage	

125 Gift Ideas, Not Including the Tie

Lamp

Lap desk

Large print newspaper

Laundry basket

Leather photo album

Leg warmers

Lightweight golf bag

Lumberjack shirt

Lush terrycloth bathrobe

Magazine subscription

Make-up mirror

Map of the heavens

Model train

Monthly grapefruit deliveries

Museum membership

Ostrich-feather duster

Pair of goldfish

Pasta maker

Peppermint lozenges

Personalized baseball bat

Personalized stationery

Pet toys

Petits fours

Picnic basket

Pink bath towel

Pipe rack

Plaid blanket

Portable electronic typewriter

Potpourri sachets

Roller skates

Radio

Rubber stamps

Shakespeare's sonnets

Shoe trees

Side of smoked salmon

Ski goggles

Software game

Stepladder

Straw hat

Striped leotard

Sweatshirt

Set of English hairbrushes

Tarragon vinegar

Teapot

Telephone calling card

Ten dollars in currency of traveler's destination

Tennis ball machine

Tennis racket

Tent

Terra-cotta flower boxes

Textured wool stockings

Tobacco sampler

Travel-size cosmetics

Two pounds of homemade cookies

Two 26-inch-square European pillows

Umbrella

Underwater camera

Waterproof sportwatch

Weekend at spa

Wide-mouth toaster

Wildflower seeds

Wine rack

Wok

Wooden blocks

World atlas

Wrap travel jewelry case

Zodiac computer

ROCK-A-BYE KITTY: In the late 1800s, Margaret Getschell, superintendent of Macy's department stores, taught a pair of cats (dressed in doll clothes) to lie still in cribs in the toy department. The training program took a week.

WHO: _____

\# _____

_____

_____

_____

WHO: _____

\# _____

_____

_____

_____

WHO: _____

\# _____

_____

_____

_____

WHO: _____

\# _____

_____

_____

_____

WHO: _____

\# _____

_____

_____

_____

WHO: _____

\# _____

_____

_____

_____

WHO: _____

\# _____

_____

_____

_____

WHO: _____

\# _____

_____

_____

_____

Sizes and Preferences

WHO:

\#

WHO:

\#

BRIGHT IDEA: Merchandising genius John Wanamaker got hold of Thomas Edison shortly after the first public demonstration of the light bulb, and contracted to have his Philadelphia department store lit by electricity. On the fateful day in 1878, a crowd gathered to watch the store blow up, and even when it didn't, many customers wouldn't set foot inside for weeks.

WHO:

\#

WHO:

\#

WHO:

\#

WHO:

\#

WHO:

\#

SOME THINGS NEVER CHANGE: The first coin minted in New York, a copper penny, bore on its face the date, 1787, and the legend "Mind Your Own Business."

AT LEAST IT WASN'T A PHONE BILL: Seroco, North Dakota, is named for the first piece of mail to arrive at its post office: the Sears, Roebuck catalog.